ADEPTS OF THE FIVE ELEMENTS

ADEPTS
OF THE FIVE
ELEMENTS

David Anrias

WEISERBOOKS
Boston, MA/York Beach, ME

Published in 2000 by
Red Wheel/Weiser, LLC
P. O. Box 612
York Beach, ME 03910-0612

Originally published in 1933 by Routledge and Kegan
Paul, Ltd., London.

Library of Congress Cataloging-in-Publication Data

Anrias, David.
    Adepts of the five elements / David Anrias.
        p. cm.
    ISBN 1-57863-204-8 (pbk. : alk. paper)
    1. Astrology. I. Title.
BF1701 .A58 2000
133.5—dc21   00-032082

Printed in the United States of America
NP

The paper used in this publication meets the minimum
requirements of the American National Standard for
Information Sciences—Permanence of Paper for Printed
Library Materials Z39.48-1992(R1997).

CONTENTS

		PAGE
PREFACE	. . . . . .	xi
THE CHANGING AGE	. . . .	17
ADEPTS OF THE EARTH	. . . .	26
ADEPTS OF THE WATER	. . . .	37
ADEPTS OF THE AIR	. . . .	48
ADEPTS OF THE FIRE	. . . .	60
ADEPTS OF THE ETHER	. . . .	74
APPENDIX	. . . . . .	85

PREFACE

In these chaotic times, when even the most enterprising modern mind is at a loss to know in what to believe or how to act with foresight and decision, when the old standards and conventions are being abandoned and nothing has as yet been found to take their place, it is not surprising that most of us are bewildered and speculate upon the possible cause of upheavals affecting every race and every country.

Only to students of occultism or astrology is this situation in some degree comprehensible ; for they realise that the world has entered upon a new cycle in which old traditions of living must inevitably give way before the forces of a New Era which are even now becoming manifest all the world over.

Through contact with the Masters of Wisdom and by means of astrology, I have been able in some measure to detect the causes of this general disruption as well as to foreshadow some of the subsequent developments likely to become evident, especially in the West.

The method by which this occult knowledge
has been acquired need not be described here,
as it was dealt with in detail in the preface to my
previous book, *Through the Eyes of the Masters*,
which was partly inspired with the object of
counteracting the doubt cast by Krishnamurti
upon the power of the Masters to further the
evolution of mankind.

The immediate response to this book has
justified a further endeavour to reveal how close,
on the contrary, is Their association with man's
future development as he endeavours to comprehend the five elements which go to make up
his own nature.

This assertion demands some slight elabora-
tion. As everybody knows, man's physical body
is composed of the five physical elements—earth,
water, air, fire, and ether interpenetrating them
all. His subtler bodies—astral or emotional,
mental and Buddhic or spiritual—likewise
partake in varying degrees of the subtler aspects
of these five elements, *i.e.*, the astral being co-
related to the watery element, the mental to the
airy and etheric and the Buddhic to the fiery.
In the horoscope of each individual one element
usually predominates over the others, but the
ultimate goal of man is the attainment of

self-conscious knowledge and control of each element in turn on his upward path towards the Light.

For purposes of meditation, almost impossible amidst the conflicting thought-currents in cities, I frequently seek the seclusion of a certain lonely spot on the sea-coast ; and in this spot, where earth, air and water meet, certain Adepts have been able psychically to impress me with regard to many of those problems which beset the present age. Needless to say, this knowledge has only been given out in order that I, in turn, may share it with my fellow-seekers. Whole successions of ideas were conveyed to me in the form of comprehensive pictures, which frequently included concepts with which I was already familiar, and were finally co-ordinated on the New Moon of March, 1933, under exceptionally favourable psychic conditions. Phenomena of this sort is achieved by means of the Astral Light which is temporarily vivified by higher mental matter.

This procedure is always adopted by certain Adepts, and accomplished without speech and with the greatest possible economy of force. I have tried to retain something of the brevity and terseness of this vivid experience by eliminating every superfluous word and only stressing the essentials here and there throughout the five meditations.

As the portraits of the Masters in my previous book have caused a certain amount of bewilderment, I take this opportunity to remove the objections which have arisen in the minds of various readers. It has been asserted in a deprecating way that They all resemble each other. But is this surprising, considering that They are engaged upon the same work and acting as Members of one Great Spiritual Body? It is a recognised fact that clergymen, lawyers and actors, for instance, all tend to develop similar facial characteristics, as the result of similar work in the world. Surely this law applies equally to the Adepts.

With regard to my two illustrations in the *Vision of the Nazarene*,[1] the second of these is intended to portray the initiate Jesus working against great opposition and still hampered by a body subject to time and other karmic restrictions, hence the strained expression of the face. The single lock of hair in the portrait was also deliberate, and conveys a meaning to the intuitive. The frontispiece depicts the Lord Maitreya associating Himself with the wonderful life of Jesus and the

---

[1] By the author of *The Initiate in the Dark Cycle.*

spiritual thought-form which it created throughout the centuries that followed.

Similarly the portrait of the Master Serapis, assuming a Devic form in order to hasten the Era of the Coming Race, was not intended to be an exact likeness of His present physical body, which is maintained upon far more masculine currents of force.

In conclusion, I wish to thank Mrs. Cyril Scott for much literary assistance in co-ordinating the original notes.

LONDON,   D.A.
    August, 1933.

THE CHANGING AGE

BY the quiet sea, alone in my two-roomed hut, I sat meditating during the early hours of the morning. Outside I heard the first bird, his song attuned to the first light of day. All else was still, save for the gentle waves breaking against the beach. In the general sense of quiet I became suddenly aware of the presence of my Master, His aura permeating the place with a profound sense of peace. My mind instantly ceased to speculate upon this problem or that, but became merged in His consciousness. I was intensely aware of that rare quality possessed by Him alone, controlled power combined with a subtle mentality capable of responding to the influence of the furthest cosmic murmur ; and thus lifted, for the moment, into oneness with Him, I was enabled to see, as it were with His eyes, and to comprehend some of the underlying reasons for the present confusion.

As the earth comes under the influence of a particular zodiacal sign, mankind as a whole, for the duration of that major period or cycle, responds to its particular element. Towards the end of a given cycle, a cosmic readjustment of the four elements in their relationship to our earth is inevitable, and they become re-polarised through the chief characteristics of the zodiacal sign which is to become dominant. Therefore at this particular period which is one of transition between one dispensation and another, there is a powerful element of conflict between the passing Pisces cycle and the Aquarian cycle, which is to influence the world for the next two thousand years.

Such an important change is always anticipated by the Great Hierarchy who invisibly guide man's destiny. Certain Adepts, having acquired a great spiritual affinity with the new sign through meditating upon it several centuries in advance, become attuned to its highest rate of vibration. Similarly They acquire the power to transmute its baser elements in order to counteract, as much as is karmically permitted, the Dark Forces endeavouring to delay the advent of the New Age.

Needless to say, some of the magnetic forces pouring through the zodiacal signs have more affinity with the sign of the new Air Age than others, and the sign most likely to be athwart its development is Pisces, the influence ruling the previous cycle.

Those signs having the greatest affinity with Aquarius are Libra and Gemini, being of the same airy element, likewise Sagittarius and Aries, which are similarly in benefic aspect to it, forming a sextile instead of a trine. The two latter signs are, in addition, complementary to Aquarius, since their fiery element is easily co-related to the element air.

The magnetic forces of the two remaining signs Scorpio and Cancer, like Pisces, are not likely to have much affinity with those of Aquarius ; for Scorpio is in square or evil aspect to this sign, and Cancer is both negative and conservative, its main characteristic being a powerful inclination to cling to the past. Again the forces of the three earthy signs will prove even more of an obstruction, consisting as they do of the densest matter of all. Neither Virgo nor Capricorn have much affinity with Aquarius, whilst Taurus, being a fixed sign, is in square aspect to it and so is likely to set up the greatest resistance of all to those cosmic changes that are having a stupendous effect upon the rising generation and even upon the planet itself.

This being so, it inevitably follows that those

Adepts who are endeavouring to manipulate the spiritual forces associated with the New Age will have an exceedingly difficult task during the next few centuries, for not only have They to anticipate the future to a considerable extent, but to avoid nullifying the work of those among Their Brother Adepts, who, for the sake of the majority who still cling to traditions and old religious customs, guard the expiring forces of the passing Age. The task of these Adepts is an equally difficult one, since They are ever contending with those destructive powers who endeavour to take advantage of a changing Era to cause misery, unrest and chaos wherever possible.

Through the medium of my Master's consciousness I was enabled to realise much that had hitherto seemed obscure to me, and to so many others, with regard to that great outpouring of spiritual force at the close of a minor cycle of the Kali-Yuga about 1890, which resulted in the founding of the Esoteric Section of the Theosophical Society. As every occult student knows, a vast amount of arcane knowledge was given to the world through the great initiate H. P. Blavatsky. By an act of sacrifice on the higher planes on the part of the White Lodge, the whole aura of the earth became charged up by currents of spiritual energy. These currents began to encircle the earth at an increasingly high rate of vibration, stimulating the more sensitive types towards greater and greater efforts in their desire for spiritual wisdom. Their physical-etheric centres became more and more responsive to the influence of the higher planes, in spite of the fact that many of them were actively employed in mundane work. Needless to say, these men and women were subjected to a very great strain, such as the potential occult student or mystic of the past, who retired as a matter of course to the seclusion of temple or monastery, had never experienced. This practice of withdrawing from the world in order to contact spiritual verities through deep meditation continued throughout the Pisces cycle, the twelfth sign and the twelfth house being alike in creating the desire as well as the suitable conditions for such a life. But with the new cycle these methods could not endure, Aquarius tending to turn forces outwards instead of inwards by means of community-work and similar public activities associated with the eleventh house.

Inevitably there must be a period of transition between any two cycles, when the only possible course is to adopt methods of occult instruction combining as far as possible the old with the new. Therefore the training of the first Western group of occult students was largely coloured by Indian methods, and comprised strict instructions to be rigidly adhered to.

After Madame Blavatsky's death, Dr. Annie Besant endeavoured to maintain this same Indian discipline, which she herself had quickly mastered and scrupulously carried out in everyday life, despite the fact that she was freely mingling with people in the outside world. How far this was achieved through strength of will and how far through reverting to congenial customs associated with her immediate past life as an Indian, it is impossible to say. It soon became evident to the White Lodge that whilst an Indian initiate functioning through a Western body might quickly dominate that body through the old Indian higher vehicles retained for the purpose, it was all but impossible for the average Western occult student to maintain the old Eastern standards of physical purity under modern conditions.

Other difficulties also arose. The *Secret Doctrine* was the chief object of group-study, but the higher mental body of the average bewildered Western student was usually discovered to be insufficiently equipped for the task. Likewise early meditation on an empty stomach, often between 6 and 7 a.m., although comparatively easily sustained in India, where both long custom and climatic conditions were favourable, seemed all but impossible in the West.

About 1912 the Adepts who had sponsored the Theosophical Society realised that what was possible for an initiate possessing a powerful will as well as the means of *creating her own surrounding conditions*, was not feasible for the average Western pupil still hampered by past karma or a delicate body.

Therefore these particular Masters effected a transference of occult force, hitherto wholly confined to the higher mental plane, to the lower mental, and later to the astral plane by means of group ceremonial magic.

Naturally this transference of force involved a great sacrifice on Their part,[1] and required the co-operation of another Adept, who had been associated with purely Western methods of occult

---

[1] " Those of you who have carefully thought on these subjects will realise that while the knowledge of a Master is as regards you or me, practical omniscience, it is by no means omniscience on His own plane, relative to the problems with which He has to deal and which He has to solve. . . . Hence the possibility of *miscalculation, the possibility of error*, the possibility of mistake. . . . When, then a Master volunteers to serve as what may

training through several centuries, having retained a physical body suited to this particular type of work.

As the reason for the aforementioned change of policy was never explained, many members, imagining that it implied failure to maintain the original standards inaugurated by H. P. Blavatsky, resigned from the Society. Those who had joined it at a period when occult study pure and simple was *de rigueur*, left it, largely because their karma was not of the kind that could be worked out through ceremonial and the *group-karma* which this form of activity inevitably entails.

For the benefit of those unconversant with the technicalities of astrology, I must here point out that the element water rules the emotional or astral plane, with which ceremonial magic is closely associated. Henceforth the Theosophical Society, unconsciously for the most part, embarked upon a minor cycle demanding activities in connection with this emotional or watery element,

literally be called the scapegoat of a new spiritual movement, He takes up a karma whose whole course *He is unable to see*."—Annie Besant, *London Lectures of* 1907.

" For if one sees the Theosophical Society aright, it is as one of the builders of that coming time, the civilisation of the Sixth Root Race, with the *experiments* that will go before it in the Sixth and Seventh sub-races of the Fifth. For these *experiments* take long in the making, and, as a great teacher once said : *Time is no object with us*."—*Ibid.*

which, strange to say, predominated over all the others in the horoscope of its founding in November, 1875.[1] This astrological fact had been viewed with misgiving by some of the Adepts, who, nevertheless, with Their far-seeing eyes, saw that it would afford immediate opportunities for growth for certain types of egos.[2]

[1] "'Is the West ready for a movement of this sort again ? Can it be carried on in such an environment without doing more harm than the good which it is capable of accomplishing ?' And so much discussion arose . . . and most were against it, and declared the time was not ripe; . . . as the question of time is always one of the most complicated questions for Those who have to deal with the great law of cycles and the evolution of man, it was felt that it was possible that the effort might succeed, even although the time was not quite ripe, the clock had not quite struck the hour." —*London Lectures of* 1907, by Annie Besant, page 126.

[2] The horoscope of the Theosophical Society is given in the appendix to this book, together with that of Annie Besant, C. W. Leadbeater, Krishnamurti and H. P. Blavatsky, in specific relation to it.

ADEPTS OF THE EARTH

NEPTUNE, associated at its highest with spiritual love and the mystical element in Christianity, was entering the earthy sign Taurus at the time of the founding of the Theosophical Society, thus considerably mitigating the uncompromising and stubborn element of that sign, and creating conditions in which reincarnated mystics of the past might recover some of their old memories and religious experiences. The fact that Neptune is the *only* planet in an earthy sign is also significant, inasmuch as it gives but little scope for the gratification of personal ambition, and creates a tendency to turn inward, in order to contact the higher planes through meditation.

Through personal devotion to the Master Jesus during the Christian era, certain egos have developed this power of meditation to a fine point. For such as these, ceremonies are not necessary, neither do they feel impelled to express themselves through service.

Instinctively, in their present incarnation, they are drawn towards cathedrals or the ancient churches of the past, and the Master Jesus becomes for them a living reality during meditation, as they contemplate the exquisite stained-glass windows, depicting His life of sacrifice. Here in these sacred places where the earth is blessed, they dimly sense that the astral or emotional element is stilled, subordinated to the vibration of that Great Adept who guards the heart of the mystic and the active devotee alike.

The life of the pupil who is approaching the path through mysticism is usually so planned that he is able to remain in one place during the difficult process of learning to still the mind and make it responsive to the influence of his Master. Often he is unconsciously drawn to a centre which has been previously magnetised by an initiate of his own nationality, as it is much easier to tune-in to the Master through the particular occult rate of vibration of one's own country than through that of another.

When the mystic has perfected his faculty of inner response to his Master, he is able to contact Him no matter what his surrounding conditions, and here the passivity of the mystic becomes merged into the activity of the occultist.

Whilst meditating upon the influence of the aforementioned magnetised centres, I was transported in thought by my Master to the old Chelsea church in the vicinity of which, before leaving for the East, I had undergone my own mystical training, and whither I had afterwards returned to complete it in a more positive sense.

He conveyed to me that wherever a great initiate has endeavoured to realise for himself some of the fundamental truths of occultism, the ground about his dwelling-place takes on something of his magnetic and spiritual quality. Indeed, it is not too much to say that the physical-etheric conditions created by such a one may persist for several centuries after his death.

The Chelsea church and the ground near by, which used to be a beautiful garden bordering the river, thus still retain something of the vibrations of Sir Thomas More, who lived there for a considerable time before enduring the martyrdom so frequently the lot of the initiate who dies for the sake of some ideal beyond the comprehension of his contemporaries. Through being in touch with these conditions I contacted something of the personality of this remarkable man, who combined the inner powers of the mystic with the trained brain of the executive thinker ; and later on I began to realise that His living presence still overshadows this magnetised spot. I sensed the same restrained and disciplined mind awaiting that time when England will be capable of responding to occult leadership inspired from Higher Sources. In anticipation of this development, various centres magnetised by Him in the past are kept guarded in order that certain advanced egos who have karmic associations with England, may at some future time be enabled to make an etheric or even a physical contact with the English Adepts who guide the destiny of their race.

At these centres, if they have developed a sufficient degree of clairaudience, they will receive occult training suitable for their work in the outer world. Those whose past karma permits them to become more sensitive and acquire a certain amount of clairvoyance, will be entitled to an occult exposition of the general plan of the national future, which, as they will be impressed, must be kept in mind during their work in the present.

In this connection it was also shown to me that many of those egos, who, either as kings or in other positions of authority have made important links with a particular country, reincarnate

in that country in order to raise it up
and to work out that specific form of karma
which can only be generated in positions of
responsibility.

After this brief glimpse into the future of my
own race, my thoughts were led back to the
present ; I realised that the most advanced types
were responding to the Uranian influence now
everywhere operative and tending to develop an
international spirit in all the leading cities of the
West. With the ever-increasing facilities for
travel, with the wide-flung effects of the radio
and the translation of successful plays and films
into several languages, a new cosmopolitan view-
point has become evident everywhere ; this is
reflected in the art, the literature and even the
architecture of the age, since the huge *Atlantean*
structures of New York are being repeated
on a smaller scale in every city of the
world.

It was shown to me that this ever-increasing
international spirit has been much fostered by the
Master Rakoczi, His marvellous mind behind
every activity and trend of thought.

In the field of politics, He is especially active,
particularly in those countries which might prove

a danger to their neighbours and precipitate war. Often at times of crisis He will counteract such tendencies by impressing with sudden and illuminating suggestions the minds of those few statesmen who are capable of responding to His Uranian personality. I saw that it will not be long before a group of such men will combine to bring about world-peace and evolve a comprehensive Uranian scheme in order to maintain it, thereby creating entirely new political standards for their successors.

My Master then conveyed to me that the vibrations of Uranus and Neptune are far too high to influence the average man of to-day without becoming distorted as soon as they come into contact with his imperfectly co-ordinated vehicles. The close opposition of these two planets lasting for several years within comparatively recent times, precipitated upon the earth great spiritual forces which, as the majority of mankind were not sufficiently evolved to utilise them, became expressed in various ways as intensification of egoism.

Amongst other undesirable manifestations, an enormous increase in homo-sexuality became apparent, Uranus being associated with the positive side of sex-perversion,[1] and Neptune with the negative. Their reverse lunar motion is connected with this development and tends to make those who respond to the lower influence of these planets intensely individualistic through a re-polarisation of the astral and etheric bodies. The emotions in consequence seek a twisted and distorted form of expression,[2] and there is an increasing desire for new and strange sensations to be gratified at all costs. This re-polarisation is also considerably enhanced by the fact that Uranus tends to govern the minds of men and the emotions of women, whilst Neptune often sways the emotions of men and the minds of women.[3]

Each sex, instead of finding its complement in the other, becomes frustrated and turned inwards on itself through the powerful *reverse* lunar motion of these two planets, the vibrations of which are frequently used to precipitate karma of an

[1] " In marriage and love-affairs, Uranus can be particularly evil through its self-assertion. There is no ' give and take ' because of intense individuality, and the *positive* types of sexual perversion, homo-sexuality, etc., associated with this planet are all due to the same tendency, which may cause great cruelty through self-assertion or produce the homo-sexual condition through the extreme intensification of the self."—Vivian E. Robson, B.Sc., *Modern Astrology*, 1924.

[2] This delicate subject has been more comprehensively dealt with in *The Initiate in the New World*.

[3] See *The Art of Synthesis*, page 121, Alan Leo.

emotional nature in order that the ego may become free of all personal desires in future lives.

Nevertheless, it is possible even in the present incarnation for both men and women, by rising above sex-desire, to contact the higher vibrations of Uranus and Neptune.   The old Greek method of sublimation through metaphysical aspiration[1] is still the only door by which man can attain to true spiritual union, and this applies equally to the woman of the future, who will find herself better equipped for this method of development than her less enterprising forebears.

During the next few centuries the physical-etheric centres of both sexes will undergo considerable alteration, a state of transition which invariably precedes the inception of a new Root-Race.

My Master now showed me certain pictures of past civilisations and super-imposed them upon those connected with the present.   I was able to see in the brief space of time allotted to me how the different races were evolved and differentiated from each other simply by means of the *order of vitalisation* of their physical-etheric centres.

In the case of the Fourth Root-Race, the life-force was directed from the solar plexus to the throat, thence to the head and finally to the heart-

---

[1] See *The Initiate in the Dark Cycle*, Routledge.

c

centre. Towards the end of the Atlantean civilisation this development frequently ceased at the head-centre, with the result that at that time black magicians were in the majority. In order to counteract this tendency in His new race, Vaivasvata, the Manu or Ruler of the New Fifth Root-Race, *reversed* the order of vitalisation, beginning with the heart, then the throat, then the head and finally the solar plexus. Apparently this Fifth-Race line of development also has disadvantages, inasmuch as the solar plexus, the last to be vitalised, has been neglected, and thus innumerable difficulties which in modern parlance are termed complexes have arisen. In the East this solar plexus centre is called the *Web of Life*,[1] and there is a tradition—handed down from the First Sub-Race of the Fifth Root-Race, during the time when the new Race was desperately trying to free itself from the expiring influence of Atlantis—that this centre must be avoided at all costs and negotiated only by the Guru. This tradition obtains to the present day, and it is therefore *in the West* that, with the beginning of the new Sixth Sub-Race, a tentative effort to comprehend this centre is being made under the inspiration of certain Adepts.

[1] Associated with the signs Libra and Virgo-Scorpio.

Thus the *modus operandi* of psycho-analysis creates a form of mental-astral-etheric activity which descends from the brain into the solar plexus, and will ultimately ascend to the heart-centre when the subconscious has been finally understood and *controlled*. In this way the new line of development will differ from *both* the preceding ones.

The danger of this present method, however, lies therein that instead of being raised to the superconscious mind within the heart-centre, the life-force having once *descended*, may *remain* concentrated in the subconscious, where everything is seen solely in terms of phallic symbols.

This descent is not only manifest in psycho-analysis but in the whole trend of modern thought ; in the more discordant types of modern music, which tend to stir the barbaric elements in the subconscious ; in modern painting where much the same is apparent through the deliberate use of primitive form and colour ; and finally in modern literature through the ruthless analysis of desire of every kind, entirely divorced *as yet* from all tenderness.

As further regards psycho-analysis itself, just as Uranus is associated with the mental side, Neptune influences the more sympathetic element of this science, and enables the analyst to identify himself with his patient.

Needless to say, if this identification is too much emphasised, the patient becomes utterly dependent on the analyst. To counteract this tendency the development of the *will* side of Uranus is essential in order that the patient may take over full control of the subconscious mind *himself*, thus in the course of time making it possible to dispense with extraneous analysis altogether.

I also saw that between 1938-1941, when these two planets will be in benefic aspect to each other from the earthy signs Taurus and Virgo, an old Atlantean method of uniting the will with the subconscious mind will be re-discovered by an initiate and practised by a group of occult students, only at a higher point of the spiral, and that when properly employed, this method will promote harmony and stability throughout Man's vehicles, rendering him a more competent and fitting instrument for the service of the Masters.

ADEPTS OF THE WATER

A T this point my Master showed me other pictures relating to the element water and the astral plane, and I was enabled to see the Master Rakoczi's endeavours throughout past centuries to spiritualise mediæval Europe. Transposed, as it were, on to this new current, I realised that because it is the destiny of Western civilisation to evolve along lines of conscious co-operation, it became essential that this aspiration should be attempted, even in occultism, by the advanced members of the race. In order to facilitate this and to create a method of occult discipline suitable for Europe, the Master Rakoczi reincarnated century after century in the West, experiencing all the physical limitations of each period, first as a mystic and then as an occultist. During the second stage, he adapted some of the ancient Egyptian occult ceremonial into a form suitable to the times.

Unfortunately, these earlier attempts to materialise a real sense of brotherhood upon earth,

chiefly associated with the Masonic and Rosi-
crucian Orders, failed again and again, mainly
because so many of the members desired individual
knowledge or power rather than that enlighten-
ment which is only attained through occult
service.

Egos on the seventh or ceremonial Ray tend
to be drawn, life after life, into the Masonic
Order or other kindred activities of the period.
This is partly due to an egoic urge to succeed in
selfless collective magic, and partly to some inner
sense of previous failure. The activities of a
group whose members have not as yet learnt to
control their own emotional desires nor the forces
invoked by ceremonial, generate a subtle form of
karma which, in its turn, can only be worked out
through a group. Hence these souls are drawn
automatically towards such activities as afford
them scope to repeat past tendencies or to make
good past errors.

There was, of course, an astrological explanation
for this new development of the Theosophical
Society along seventh Ray lines. The progressed
Jupiter, the planet of ceremonial, was applying
to the conjunction of the radical Sun in the fifth
house, the house esoterically associated with past
karma. Later on, this planet also formed a

benefic trine aspect to the mid-heaven containing Pisces, the sign of the passing Age, and caused a period of general expansion, particularly associated with ceremonial.

By an extraordinary concatenation, these forces involving the element water, hitherto associated with the previous Age, were also utilised to herald a new Era, for about this period Dr. Annie Besant proclaimed Krishnamurti as the potential medium of the World Teacher.

That these forces of the old line and the new might possibly conflict with each other was never seriously considered. It was almost universally assumed that in some miraculous fashion " new wine could be poured into old bottles " without ultimate disaster. How Krishnamurti, whose horoscope was polarised chiefly towards the future, would be likely to react to the various activities of the Society based exclusively upon the past, was a question for the astrologer alone ; by everyone else it was taken for granted that he would somehow evolve a teaching wholly new and stimulating, whilst at the same time *never* athwart the existing ceremonial *régime*, which by 1925, the year when the Jupiterian conjunction was at full strength, was completely dominating the Society.

Because the horoscope of the Theosophical Society consists of planets forming opposition and square aspects to each other from the four fixed signs and the four elements, thereby creating a cross in the heavens, it is an exceedingly interesting one and has a special application to the subject of this book, *i.e.*, the conflict of the elements at certain periods of man's evolution on this planet.

This horoscope is a very powerful one, inevitably affecting in varying degrees each individual occult student as he joins the Society. What the precise effects are, depends, of course, on whether the mutual aspects between his own nativity and that of the Society are benefic or otherwise.

The nativity of Dr. Besant, for instance, formed many benefic aspects to that of the Society, her Jupiter and Uranus vitalising and inspiring numerous physical plane activities through their conjunction to the ascendant and mid-heaven respectively. These aspects expanded the Society in a physical sense and at the same time stimulated Dr. Besant's own spiritual development on every plane.

With Krishnamurti the opposite was the case, his planets either forming a conjunction with the original cross from fixed signs, thereby enhancing its original difficulties, or else falling in the twelfth house, the house of self-undoing and introspection.

It was, therefore, a foregone conclusion to the astrological student that the future was not likely to materialise as anticipated by the majority. To those who find this whole situation inexplicable, there can only be offered the following elucidation.

Spiritual growth is only obtained through the transmutation of so-called malefic aspects ; the path of occultism cannot be approached through a horoscope consisting of benefic aspects alone, such as might create conditions for a pleasant holiday or period of relaxation. The Theosophical Society was founded upon this significant combination of planets and elements because *only* such a configuration would be powerful enough to precipitate all personal karma from past lives in order that its members might be entirely free to work for the Masters in future incarnations.

This is demonstrated by the fact that the majority of the planets in the original horoscope are in Scorpio and in the house of the past in malefic aspect to those in Aquarius, on the cusp of the house of the future. Such a configuration denotes that past *complexes, ceremonial, sex or otherwise,* remain to be worked out in various ways before each unit in the corporate body of the Society can contact the forces of the New Age.

Various articles, anticipating the present situation, appeared in *The Theosophist* between the years 1920 and 1925, written under the inspiration of my Master, who wished to convey in advance that the stars in their courses could not wholly be ignored.

About the same period the new psycho-analytical point of view, wholly Uranian and ruthless in its detachment, began to influence the intelligentsia of the West. This science, originally inspired among numerous other activities by a certain Adept, became more widely diffused, influencing many types of people, especially among the younger generation. It was not long before its basic ideas came also to be accepted by certain occult students, who began to criticise leading initiates from this new angle of thought.

Messages alleged to be inspired by the Masters through the medium of this or that advanced initiate, were no longer instantly accepted, but were subjected to the devastating query as to whether they had *really* emanated from the Masters, or merely from the depths of the particular initiate's subconscious mind. It was evident that by this new menace, the old occult authority of the Society had become shaken. Uranus, the destroyer, was ruthlessly completing his work, for never can students of the present or future approach occultism by the same Saturnian path as their forebears.

It became evident to the Adepts, ever watching over the world, that the younger members of the Society were responding far more to the revolutionary Uranian element latent in the sign Aquarius than to the Saturnian ; similarly that a discipline imposed from without, rather than from within, must inevitably fail to develop individual initiative which is the peculiar characteristic of the planet Uranus, ruler of the New Age.

This conflict between the forces of the old Age and those of the new, so marked within the Theosophical Society, was even more apparent in the outside world. The younger generation expressed active criticism of and revolt against the traditions and ideals of the older generation, although they had as yet not evolved anything of a more positive nature to take their place. The influence of these young people was wholly destructive, as they were responding to the Shiva side of Uranus, rather than to its creative aspect.

In short, with the conjunction of Mars and Uranus in 1909 and after, the etheric currents associated with the occult development of the past began to disperse. On Uranus entering *its own sign Aquarius, the world war was precipitated, prior to the reinforcement of the earth by new cosmic etheric currents from beyond the solar system.* And on entering Pisces, Uranus was used to precipitate on to the astral plane *these same cosmic etheric forces*, thereby disintegrating everything that could obstruct the commencement of the New Era.

Every plane of consciousness now being subjected to hitherto alien influences emanating from high cosmic sources, the Master Rakoczi became chiefly concentrated upon the immediate difficulty of guarding His pupils from the machinations of the Dark Forces ; these Forces, as previously implied, always seeking to take advantage of the revolutionary effects produced by certain etheric innovations and their inevitable reactions upon the rapidly altering astral element. He realised that as regards the younger people the whole polarisation of the higher vehicles was being changed as they unconsciously adapted themselves to the new psychic conditions, while the older people whose various bodies were far more set, found it increasingly difficult to accomplish a similar adaptation. Some among them who endeavoured to manipulate the forces associated with the old line of ceremonial, still active within the Theosophical Society, became conscious of an ever-decreasing response as they performed certain rites of magic. Moreover, those who persisted in doing so, despite certain occult warnings which were wrongly interpreted or completely ignored, began to suffer physical reaction owing to the fact that the etheric plane, the intermediary between the astral and the physical, was also in such a chaotic condition.

Because of these stupendous changes affecting the astral plane or watery element, the Master Rakoczi, in order to safeguard His pupils and also the better to direct some of His more pressing political activities, temporarily withdrew to the mental plane. He perforce abandoned certain astral currents and centres of force as well as those forms of ceremonial and words of power which He had previously vitalised, since they had become exploited for wrong ends by a secret organisation.

This organisation had not remained satisfied with endeavouring to control the religion of the West, but for several centuries had utilised and debased its knowledge and control of the thought-currents in order to enter the field of politics.[1] Thus its members repeatedly handicapped the Master Rakoczi in His efforts to improve the constitutional laws and general conditions of Europe.

Whenever a potential pupil, under inspiration from the higher planes, endeavoured to contend against the reactionary tendencies of his time, by opening up new lines of mental development, he inevitably became the focus of the combined thought of the above-mentioned organisation, bènt upon his ultimate destruction.

This was undoubtedly true in the case of the Crown Prince Rudolf of Austria, for instance, who strove to foster a more enlightened point of view than that dominating the rigid Austrian Court, and for so doing was ceaselessly harassed by the intrigues of these hidden enemies. In how far these were responsible for his actual death must remain an open question.[2] Suffice it to say

[1] For a more detailed history of the machinations of this body, see *The Vision of the Nazarene*, by the author of *The Initiate in the Dark Cycle*.

[2] This terrible tragedy closed the door for any further occult experiments on the part of the Master Rakoczi as far as Austria was concerned, another sign indicating that Neptune, the planet of democracy, and not Jupiter, has the greater affinity with the passing age. Since then one throne after another associated with Rome and its strict ceremonial *régime* has fallen, whilst more and more the younger generation of princes are marrying commoners.

that it is known that his life out of the body in
the inner world has been a preparation in order
that in a future incarnation he may become one
of the pioneers of the new race.

It is such as he who, having sacrificed worldly
ambition and died putting love before all else,
become channels for the rare force emanating
from the Buddhic or plane of spiritual love—that
lofty plane whence the future race will draw its
inspiration, thereby responding to the influence
of the planet Neptune.

ADEPTS OF THE AIR

SUDDENLY the pictures vanished and I became conscious once more of the beauty of my immediate surroundings. Outside the thrush had ceased singing, and the sun was rising over the calm sea. The delightful weather, the wide expanse of sky, merging into the low undulating hills beyond the marsh flats in the foreground, became a perfect setting for what I had just experienced. A solitary lark near by soared upwards, his song becoming fainter as he floated out of sight. I began to feel the vibrations change. The serene, steady rhythm of my Master gradually merged into another exquisite vibration with the appearance of the Master Serapis. Several Air Devas accompanied Him, and the air became vibrant with their presence. I sensed rather than saw these Devas as tall columns of brilliant white light assuming geometrical shapes of rarest beauty and purest mathematical exactitude ; and I understood them to belong to the Uranian type directed by Lords of Karma to break up old forms in order that higher ones may come to birth in a new age.

It was conveyed to me by the Master Serapis that the Aquarian Age will be divided into three periods or cycles, each lasting about seven hundred years.

The first or Uranian cycle, will, of necessity, be a period of rapid changes and considerable destruction. Therefore, at this time the First Ray Devas will perforce take precedence of all others.

I saw that in a few centuries all interest in the *old* forms of ceremonial will apparently have died out,[1] the majority being interested in psychic phenomena, but approached from a more scientific point of view than to-day. I also saw how the Air Devas will be increasingly active in helping man to make his bodies more and more responsive to the forces of the air, and hence more intuitive and open to the influence of the higher mental plane.

During the Gemini or second decanate of Aquarius the advance-guard of humanity will have acquired the power to control the forces of

---

[1] See *Man, Whence, How and Whither*, by Annie Besant and C. W. Leadbeater, page 456.

D

the denser sub-divisions of etheric matter—a
subject with which I shall deal more comprehensively later. I saw a magnificent race being
evolved, self-conscious in the etheric centres,
gradually acquiring complete control over each
in turn, but in a *different order* of vitalisation from
that experienced by those Fifth-Race initiates
who acquired control in previous eras, when
other attributes of consciousness required a
different kind of vitalisation. This new order
was inaugurated by the First Ray Devas under
the instruction of certain Adepts soon after the
commencement of the Aquarian Age ; it was,
however, regarded somewhat doubtfully and even
denounced by lesser initiates and clairvoyants
whose past karma and present bodies made it
impossible for them to contact the new forces
without considerable risk, their kundalini having
been already awakened in the *old* way.

The Uranian or First Ray influence having
during the first few centuries destroyed the old
method of occult training and inaugurated the
new, the gentler Second or Mercurian Ray will
take over the guiding of the Geminian cycle.
Finally, I glimpsed the whole of humanity becoming responsive to the three highest Rays
during the final sub-cycle of Aquarius, a period

when man and woman alike will have complete control of the sympathetic system as well as the ability to create by means of thought-power in mental etheric matter. During this period the influence and power of sound will be generally recognised. Through my contact with the consciousness of the Master Serapis, I was able to obtain some idea of the music of that distant period, which, with its subtle combinations of sound, its third-tones and its quarter-tones, will demand for its full appreciation an entirely new musical sense.[1]   In some respects, however, I recognised that this music of the future resembled the highest type of Ancient Indian music, in that it tended to liberate the higher bodies from the limitations of the physical plane.

I then saw that the general knowledge of occult law, combined with that of the power of sound, will render the merging of the Aquarian Age into the Capricornian more harmonious than the present period of transition.

With my realisation of this fact, the pictures began to fade, but as the Master Serapis was about to leave me, He emphasised the fact that

---

[1] This subject has been further elaborated by Cyril Scott in his book, *Music, Its Secret Influence throughout the Ages*, Rider & Co.

men and women of to-day can only hope *physically*
to respond to the higher forces of the New Age
if their vehicles respond to the element Air, and
there remains little or no karma to be worked out
through other elements.

Reflection upon the comparative ease with
which the Aquarian Age would merge into the
Capricornian, the sign always associated with
India and her ancient occult traditions, led my
thoughts back to the present. I realised that the
position was reversed in more ways than one, for
nowadays, owing to the ever-increasing influence
of Aquarius, the average occult student is finding
it all but impossible to maintain the Capricornian
traditions.

This interesting conflict between the two signs
can be seen reflected in the progressed horoscope
of the Theosophical Society. In 1909 its progressed Sun entered Capricorn in conjunction
with the radical mid-heaven of Dr. Besant's
nativity. She had already, as President of the
Society, made Adyar her headquarters and had
just discovered an Indian boy as the future medium
of the World Teacher. Henceforth the Theosophical Society embarked upon a minor Capricornian cycle of thirty years, during which time

India continued to be the country towards which every member looked for inspiration.

Between 1937 and 1938 the progressed Moon in the horoscope of the Society will be in malefic aspect to Mars, Saturn and Uranus in turn. It is obvious that these years will be years of great stress, heralding another thirty-year cycle during which, with the progressed Sun's entry into Aquarius, the Society as a whole will become more responsive to the sign of the New Age. That this period is likely to be an exceedingly difficult one is shown by the fact that the progressed Sun afflicts both the radical Moon and Neptune as he enters the sign Aquarius.

The Moon, ruler of the ascendant, Cancer, in the radical horoscope, is a very important influence in the map as a whole ; and each time it has progressed over one of the points of the fixed sign cross which make up the original nativity, it has precipitated one crisis or another within the Society.

Let us cite a few of the most striking examples. The first time the progressed Moon was passing through Scorpio and in malefic aspect to Mars, Saturn and Uranus in turn, the Coulomb scandal materialised, involving Madame Blavatsky, owing to the fact that the Moon was also in malefic aspect to her radical planets in Leo and Aquarius.

While the progressed Moon was in *Capricorn* and in benefic aspect to the radical Sun, the Esoteric Section was founded.

During its period in Aquarius, however, once more in malefic aspect to Mercury, Jupiter, Uranus and the Sun in turn, the Judge secession occurred.

The next time it entered Scorpio was coincident with the numerous law-cases in connection with the guardianship of Krishnamurti.

In its second passage through Aquarius it created further difficulties, but this time through the controversy that arose with regard to the Liberal Catholic Church.

Whilst in 1931, when the progressed Moon was in conjunction with Uranus, in the heart sign Leo and in *exact opposition* to Krishnamurti's radical ascendant and the *radical Saturn* of the Theosophical nativity, it forced the Society to face up to a test with regard to its belief in the Masters—that belief which, as goes without saying, is the corner-stone of the entire organisation.

What may we then anticipate when the *Sun* also forms powerful aspects to the radical planets in fixed signs during 1938-41, 1944-46,

1954-56, 1957-59 and 1962-64 ? Surely these years will be used to precipitate upon the Theosophical Society the new Aquarian teachings —Aquarius ruling the radical eighth and ninth, the houses of occultism ? I venture to prognosticate that during the above years there will be evolved a *new* occult method of approaching *old* problems, especially in connection with the sign Scorpio, and necessitating even further tests and adaptations on the part of the members of that period.

At this point I became conscious of the exquisite vibration emanating from the presence of the Master Koot Hoomi. Enfolding me within His love-filled aura, He impressed upon me again that this period within the Theosophical Society which I have just astrologically foreshadowed, must be regarded from the standpoint of the Adepts and seen not merely as one of conflict and trial, but as one in which glorious opportunities will be offered each individual unit to face the limitations and hindrances in his own nature, to conquer and eliminate undesirable tendencies, to transmute power used perchance mistakenly in the past, into that power of Love which can never again be perverted for evil ends

. . . in short, to burn up all that may be of dross in the lower nature so that the higher may emerge untramelled, victorious and joyous. . . .

Needless to say, this way of transmutation cannot be accomplished nor even approached without suffering ; some there may be who will fall by the wayside. But those who have the courage to endure, to fight, and above all *to face themselves*, may rest in the assurance that not for one instant will they be left to struggle alone. Though *apparently* solitary and in darkness, their every step and every effort is noted by Those who watch over them, but who *may not* karmically, and in any case *would not* intervene, since They realise that alone through this persistent individual struggle may that spiritual growth be attained which is veritably the crown of all endeavour.

Nevertheless, since They recognise that the problems of the new Age are peculiarly complex, involving as they do a different polarisation of spiritual force on every plane, a certain amount of extraneous assistance is permitted by the Lords of Karma. And thus Master Koot Hoomi and His Brother Morya will make on the inner planes the sacrifice of identifying certain of Their vehicles of consciousness with those of some advanced pupils who, during the aforementioned thirty-year cycle, will endeavour to evolve a new bridge between the Adepts and the outside world.

It was permitted me to see something of what this great sacrifice on the part of the Adepts will involve. I realised that whereas formerly, under the Capricornian *régime*, the Master would occasionally overshadow the pupil, thereby for the moment raising that pupil's consciousness to His own, by the new Aquarian method the Master will assume the same rate of vibration as that of the pupil and identify Himself with his consciousness, becoming for the time being subject to the same limitations. This *modus operandi* will enable the Adepts to contact modern conditions through modern mediums, and to stimulate the study of modern problems from a modern angle ; thus the Theosophical Society, under such inspiring leadership, will once again be in the vanguard of psychological research.

It will, then, become evident that the Society, as a whole, will be raised up from the watery or emotional element into the airy element, associated with the mental plane and all activities of an artistic and intellectual nature.

By adopting the aforementioned method of psychological identification with Their pupils, the two great Adepts will furthermore be able to experience in some of Their subtler bodies the influence of Neptune and Uranus,[1] those planets which rule the future development of the Society and are likely to become increasingly potent on every plane of man's being. The fact that the ninth house, the house of the higher mind, is governed by Aquarius and Pisces, is another confirmation of this assertion, for these two signs have more affinity with Uranus and Neptune than any other planets.

Thus through great spiritual effort on all planes, the two elements water and air, in other words the emotions and the intellect, will become synthesised by contacting and harmonising the vibrations of Neptune and Uranus, so similar in their *reverse* Lunar motion and yet in all other respects so different from each other and from all the other planets in the solar system.

As in the Sociey's horoscope these two mysterious planets, together with the Moon, were rising, whereas the remainder were setting, such a position can only indicate that the former will be the dominating influences of the future, whilst the latter must inevitably become the restrictive forces of past karma.

The influences of the future involve the study

---

[1] See *Through the Eyes of the Masters*, p. 63.

of an element other than water and air, for Neptune
is still within the radius of the fiery sign Aries,
whilst the Moon and Uranus are in the fiery heart
sign Leo.

The key to the horoscope is thus to be found in
the highest of the four elements, the fire, as is
also the way to the Masters.

The inner significance of the Moon, ruler of
the ascendant, passing from the *watery* sign
Cancer into the *fiery* sign Leo, was expressed by
my Master when He spoke of those potential
pupils who would contact His brother Morya.

"Those noble souls who are capable of con-
trolling and transmuting *every desire, every emotion*, in order to attain some great ideal, respond
to the higher vibration of Mars.[1]   The whole
sympathetic system, in their case, is polarised to
that centre within the heart which answers to the
call of Service.   The astral body is raised to the
Buddhic plane through the transmuting fire of
selfless action.   Great soldiers and organisers
frequently take this line, and through their self-
sacrifice become pupils of my Brother Morya.
Meditate upon Him if you would comprehend
something of the lofty aims which He is ever seeking to inspire in the leading minds of to-day."[2]

[1] Mars rules the astral body.
[2] *Through the Eyes of the Masters*, p. 28.

ADEPTS OF THE FIRE

MY Master now showed me a picture of those centres in the heart which are co-related to other centres in the physical body. I realised that when the fire element predominates in the horoscope and consequently also in the heart centre, then, manifesting as self-sacrifice, it goes upwards as is the way of fire, to the head centre, which is under the rulership of Mars in Aries ; but should the watery or emotional element predominate in the nativity, then the force frequently becomes associated with Scorpio, also under the rulership of Mars, but goes *downwards* manifesting as sex power.

Thus the watery element in the inner worlds tends, as on this plane, to extinguish the fire. Put briefly, the battle of the soul is between raising the consciousness to spiritual fire, Buddhi, or remaining in the watery or desire-world at the mercy of innumerable conflicting forces.

But it was also shown to me that those who have the majority of planets in watery signs, frequently have the opportunity of transmuting the desire-nature and raising it to the Buddhic or fire element, by means of the *progressed* horoscope. Thus the planets leave Pisces for Aries ; Scorpio for Sagittarius ; or Cancer for Leo, as the case may be. How easy or difficult this act of transmutation, depends on the house position of the watery signs in the radical figure, for in order to make it possible at all, they should fall in *mental* houses rather than emotional, or those associated with *active* work.

My Master conveyed to me that the Master Morya was the greatest exponent of the element fire, and that He has reincarnated repeatedly as a man through the sign Aries, with but one object in view, the helping of humanity. I was shown that He scorned the lower elements and concentrated His energies entirely upon mastering the fire.

The higher Aries quality of forthgoing love to all on the part of this great Adept seeks expression in numerous ways and through many pupils, many of them quite unaware in their physical bodies of the source of their inspiration. Such pupils usually have the element fire predominating in their horoscopes, but in houses conducive to occult development on the inner planes rather than on the physical. For such types to work with people who are functioning chiefly in the *watery* element, in contradistinction to the fiery, is to court disaster, for their activities will become swamped or nullified in one way or another.

There are, however, some pupils who have karmically earned the right to have training in their physical bodies, and I realised that the tests were chiefly applied through the element fire, even when *out* of the body. Some of these First Ray pupils also have Aries strong in their horoscopes, whilst others become better expressed through Leo.[1]

It was during the conjunction of the progressed Moon to the radical Uranus in Leo in 1931, in exact opposition to Krishnamurti's ascendant, that the test through fire and the heart sign Leo —in other words, the challenge to the belief in the Masters—was applied to the Society *as a whole*. Krishnamurti being deficient in the element fire and endeavouring to express *his* interpretation of the Aquarian and airy element to the total exclusion of all others, was naturally an excellent medium for this test. And for one concentrated as he was upon acquiring self-

[1] Annie Besant had Uranus rising in Aries and W. Q. Judge the Sun and Saturn rising in that sign, whilst H. P. Blavatsky and H. S. Olcott both had Sun in Leo.

consciousness and the power to stand alone through the sign Aquarius, the outgoing activities of Leo, the opposite sign, seemed a complete waste of time.

As the Master Koot Hoomi put it in my previous book :

" Action and reaction being equal and opposite, it was inevitable that the previous period of intense outer activity,[1] propaganda and blind obedience to established authorities should be succeeded by a period of doubt and questioning of all authority. . . . Contraction must always follow expansion, in the occult world as in the material . . . Krishnamurti's teachings worked in harmony with the law of cycles in causing a contraction after a period of expansion which had already exhausted the force of the initial impulse of the last century."

From this it is evident that even the activities animated by the fire element, hitherto magnificently inspired by Dr. Besant, could not continue indefinitely, and that the forces associated with the sign Leo must take on a subtler quality, leading to a new *intuitive* power to contact the Masters *individually* rather than at second hand.

The possibility of progression from one ele-

---

[1] In the Theosophical Society.

ment into another, to which I have previously alluded, is aptly illustrated by the horoscope of the Society in which Mars is shortly leaving Pisces for Aries where it will remain until 1975. This progression points to possibilities of expansion for those on the First Ray, and indicates the way of liberation from the fixed cross of desire through the fiery element of service.[1]

Like His Brother Koot Hoomi, the Master Morya has realised the necessity of approaching modern problems from a modern angle, but He will continue to specialise in the element fire, whilst His Brother will become chiefly expressed through the element air.

In anticipation of this development, He has given out a new form of Yoga through a pupil, well known in the artistic world, but who prefers to remain anonymous in *this* connection. I came across this book some time after my own was published and found it an interesting confirmation of what I had already been told by my Master with regard to the great Adept Morya's method of training. This book *Agni Yoga* consists of aphorisms which need to be read over and over again before their inner meaning can be com-

[1] Especially during the years 1936-38, 1947-49, 1957-60 and 1961-65, when the progressed Mars forms benefic aspects to the radical Moon, Venus, Mars, Saturn and Uranus respectively.

pletely understood. Being translated from the original Sanscrit and Sensa, they do not readily find their equivalent in the English language. Nevertheless, certain sentences here and there which treat of the mastery of the element fire can be easily comprehended, and I venture to quote some of the most striking for the benefit of those who are developing along the First Ray.

For the ignorant the encounter with the elements seems a fairy-tale. But you already know how often the elements are attracted into the actual life of people.

Let us see wherein lie the similarities and differences between Agni Yoga and its preceding Yogas. Karma Yoga has many similarities with it, when it acts with the element *earth*. But when Agni Yoga masters the ways to the realisation of the *far-off worlds*, then the distinctions become apparent. Raja Yoga, Jnana Yoga, Bhakti Yoga are all isolated from their *surrounding reality*. And because of this *cannot* enter into the evolution of the future.

You may ask me what physical exercises are useful in Agni Yoga. I advise short pranayama in the morning, no longer than five minutes. One should abstain from meat, except smoked meats. Vegetables, fruit, milk and cereals are always acceptable. All wines are also barred, except for curative purposes. . . . I advise to insulate the footwear with rubber and to walk in the morning, avoiding smoking.

I speak of Fire verily existing. Not for the first

E

time does the planet experience the action of this element. During each change of races the Fire approaches as a purgatory stream.

The main thing is not to tell newcomers that the teaching of Agni Yoga is easy. Verily it is not easy. There is much strain and danger in it. . . . The mastery of the fire is a slow process. Each premature haste threatens one with conflagration. . . . Few are the trusted builders who with self-denial accept the thought of space into the chalice of the heart. They are not frightened at being scorched by the fires of the *far-off worlds*.

From where come the application and the action of the fire of Kundalini ? From the same source— the *fire of love*. . . . I love it so much, when the fire of love radiates and one can cross any obstacle !

One may remember that our enemies strongly use each spacial disturbance and try to inflict the most undesirable complications. This combination of physical and psychic conditions deserves attention.

Of course it is not easy for people of the fiery element to live in the body. But elect just these as co-workers because there is no *treason* in them. Danger will not evoke in them confusion. Duty is understood by them and the manifestation of striving *ascends like a flame*. . . . It is difficult for people to understand the signs of this element. Earth, water, air—these are evident. But that fire penetrates through water will seem as a jest. One must understand the penetration of fire. Otherwise one will not enter the fiery gates.

It would appear from this last aphorism that it is not advisable for the exponents of fire to work in conjunction with those in whom the watery element predominates. The increasing study of astrology will have as its concomitant a conscious knowledge of the elements which will be indispensable for success in even the smallest occult group-work. It will be realised that only those whose planetary influences are similar or complementary to each other should be expected to work together ; furthermore that the endeavour to coalesce an indeterminate body made up of four indeterminate elements, all more or less athwart one another, is not only futile but frequently disastrous.

The whole book seems to radiate an aura of fire, which makes it almost impossible to read it continuously. Behind the ever-youthful enthusiasm of the Master Morya one seems to sense a series of stupendous occult adventures, involving great spiritual risks, all undoubtedly connected with the inclusion of Uranus and Neptune within the limits of our Solar System. The numerous references to the *far-off worlds* and the necessity of including within one's consciousness the ever-present sense of space as a *living substance*, reveals the fact that He is even now co-relating cosmic ether with the dense physical etheric matter of our planet ; furthermore that He is also practising a type of psychological identification similar to that of His Brother Koot Hoomi, as the following quotation shows :

> The subtle body of the Yogi, liberated, visits different planes of existence. Flights into space and plunges into the *depths* of the planet are equally attainable. . . . Such realisation is needed to the progress of spirit. Such striving towards perfection will come through the *realisation of imperfection.*

These complex and daring experiments on the part of the two Brother Adepts are directly co-related to Their work in connection with Their future office as Manu and Boddhisattva of the Coming Race.

The next fiery test through the heart sign Leo for the Society repeating that of 1931, will materialise when the progressed Moon is once more in conjunction with the radical Uranus, in opposition to the radical Mars and Saturn, at the same time as the *progressed* Sun is also in conjunction with the radical Saturn. This combination of aspects will occur about 1958. Shortly after, the progressed Jupiter will enter its own sign Sagittarius in benefic aspect to the radical Moon, ruler of the ascendant, an aspect which will last until the year 2032 ! At some time during this period once more an advanced initiate and the Master Rakoczi will co-operate in inaugurating a *new* form of ceremonial, but this time co-related to the element fire instead of water.[1] It will involve the co-operation of the Fire Devas, and only those whose bodies are pure enough to become *direct* channels for this fiery force will attempt to officiate. By means of a powerful sympathetic system they will conduct the Devic force down to those unable to contact such high rates of vibration for themselves, whilst at the same time creating the vortex by means of which the Master Rakoczi may direct the aspirations of the group *upwards* through the element Fire. This Era will be one in which many pupils will reincarnate through the *mutable* fiery sign Sagittarius, as that sign confers a better equipment for co-operation with the Devas than either Aries or Leo.

To those who can identify the twelve types of the Zodiac, it is obvious that the majority of the

---

[1] " There is plenty of time for all the *experiments*, and all the blunders, and all the failures ; and all the successes of the future will grow out of these, because every failure rightly seen is the seed of a coming success."—Annie Besant, *London Lectures of* 1907.

younger generation are incarnating through Sagittarius, though as yet they are unable to respond to its higher vibrations, which create an intense aspiration to merge the individual will with that of God. For the most part the modern Sagittarian, endowed with wonderful vitality and endless opportunities to manifest physical prowess, grows dizzy with his power and misuses his gifts by over-indulgence of the senseless craving for speed tests on land, sea and in the air.

Similarly, seeing no truth in anything, he mocks at all truth. Ideals become targets for his humour, and feeling that nothing much matters, he gives himself up to this rivalry in speed, to excitement and to continual laughter. But even speed-tests have their limits, and if practised by sufficient numbers, cease to be regarded as remarkable. Likewise incessant mockery and ridicule become wearisome, and the mind inevitably turns inward upon itself, forced to seek for some underlying meaning of existence, the search for the Divine ultimately taking the place of the search for sensation.

Thus the higher side of Sagittarius will be brought into play, and by degrees those who have been such intrepid pioneers of speed on the physical plane, will become equally intrepid pioneers in the non-physical realms. In spirit and in thought they will rush out to the farthest confines of space, their very recklessness transmuted into a courage which will not shrink from the most daring cosmic experiments, their audacity tempered into a shining weapon wherewith to serve the Masters. Fearless children who have dared to play with fire and perchance been seared by it, they will learn to master and use that sacred force for the benefit of their fellows. Their freedom from inhibitions, from convention and tradition will give them a natural affinity with the Devas, and enable them to fuse their overflowing energy with these mighty forces in their numberless creative activities.

In this way the Sagittarian of the future, under the guidance of certain Adepts and Their pupils, is destined in very truth to be a pioneer, in that he will come to constitute the *first* real bridge between the Devic and the human element within our Solar system.

Much concerning this work of humanity in conjunction with the Devas has been aptly and beautifully expressed in H. K. Challoner's book, *Watchers of the Seven Spheres* : [1]

---

[1] Routledge & Sons, Ltd.

. . . In that far day the more advanced of that Sixth
    Race of men
Will have transmuted sex, conquered emotion and
    burned out all transitory desire ;
This high aim accomplished, then
Will they be taught to use the powers of mind to build
    the bodies of their children ;
And to combine in these most glorious beings the finer
    qualities of either sex :
Purified love, intuition, powerful, one-pointed will ;
Wisdom, activity—the secrets of creation, so that they
    in turn, may build in sound, colour and form.
Long must ye wait for this.
Yet even now, for him who hath eyes to see, the first
    faint signs
Of this far, promised day are manifest, for already
The beneficent gods draw mankind towards their
    goal.
Into the minds of those whose imaginations, winged by
    burning desire
To help the world, uplift them for one ecstatic instant
    into the realm of Ideation
Where time is not and the end can be perceived,
Transient flashes from this bright dawn are cast ;
Into their hands is given the torch lit by this flame
    divine, this rising sun of glory.
It is for them, whom with my burning arrow I have
    sealed to be my messengers,
To guide man's faltering steps toward this light.
It is for them, forerunners of the new age, whose eyes
    have looked into mine own,

Whose ears have heard my voice, to launch their
    brethren forth upon the great, surging tides of
    evolution ;
To be their pilot and their guiding star, drawing them
    ever upward towards the sacred heights,
The Holy Mountain, birthplace of the Race to be,
Where Man, his eyes opened, shall at last behold himself
Transfigured, glorified,
Himself no more,
But merged and one with All.

ADEPTS OF THE ETHER

DIFFICULT as it is to analyse the four elements earth, water, air and fire in their spiritual and psychic relationship to man, it is even harder to analyse the ether in a similar connection. For in the first case we have the zodiacal signs and all their associations as foci for the four elements, but in the ether there are no recognised landmarks as points of guidance, beyond the theory, accepted by Indian occultists, that it has four subdivisions, co-related to the four elements, and to the four planes, physical, astral, mental and Buddhic. Needless to say, all these subdivisions interpenetrate each other and are only distinguishable by their rates of vibration which vary in subtlety and rapidity.

The densest or lowest subdivision is that which is now recognised by science and is the medium through which the radio is active. When we listen to the wireless, we accept this invisible etheric manifestation as a matter of course, a phenomenon of science which would have been considered nothing short of a miracle a few centuries ago.

The very act of listening to the wireless tends to develop a new faculty which for the most part is almost automatic. Everyone has experienced that sensation of endeavouring for the time being to exclude sight, thought and even physical movement so that the attention may be entirely fixed upon the process of listening-in.

Something of this same method has to be adopted, but carried to a further point of concentration, in order to contact one's Master in meditation ; only instead of being entirely *negative*, the would-be chela has to make the positive effort to attune himself to a much higher rate of etheric vibration than that associated with the wireless.

It is true that the Master, in order to impress His pupil at certain important crises in his life, may sometimes descend from the heights whereon He normally functions, but the ordinary procedure is for the pupil to raise his consciousness above the rate of etheric vibration dominating the everyday life of the world. In other words, he contacts his Master on the mental plane, through that subdivision of the ether which is co-related to the element air.

This procedure is considerably facilitated by abstaining from meat and alcohol, as both are inclined to cause densification of the etheric body. Gradually the pupil becomes aware of the fact that the etheric, like the physical body, can be trained, albeit in a different way ; and that it can be made either positive or negative at will, according to what is required of it at the time.

He also realises that he must acquire control of his physical appetites, associated with the fourth or earthy subdivision of the ether, before he can become aware of or comprehend the third etheric region. Similarly that considerable understanding of the emotional difficulties of others must be acquired, before he can contact the second or airy subdivision, in which alone accurate thought-transference is possible ; and finally that the mind must be free from all personal ambition or anger before the first or fiery subdivision of the ether can be safely approached.[1]

It is this last and highest subdivision of he ether which is associated with the awakening of Kundalini within the etheric centres of the

---

[1] Each of the four subdivisions of the ether come under the influence of a different planet. According to the ancient science of numbers, the Sun has affinity with the number one, Neptune with the number two, Jupiter with the number three, and Uranus with the number four.

physical body ; but to invoke this fire without previous purification of the etheric matter associated with the lower elements and all that is correlated to them, is to run serious risks. For even assuming that the fire *does go upward* through a great and temporary effort of will and aspiration, it does so in an indeterminate manner, operating only for the time being, and may be productive of undesirable reactions.

Not one step of the ladder of occult development can be missed out with safety. This will be increasingly apparent as man becomes *self-conscious* in his etheric body as he now is in his physical one.

Further reflection upon man's future development with regard to the etheric body showed me that if greater numbers become self-conscious in etheric matter, the physical ether itself will grow far more responsive to man's volition than is now the case. This will be more apparent in some countries than in others, according to the racial etheric karma, a subject which is naturally very abstruse and one which cannot be fully elucidated here ; suffice it to say that by his efforts to control his own lower nature, man will help to transmute the lower regions of the ether and to raise up his whole country to respond to higher rates of vibration. In this work he will have the assistance and co-operation of those Etheric Devas who function in the higher subdivisions of that element.

My Master conveyed to me that as regards the knowledge and conquest of the etheric element the United States of America will soon be to the fore, partly owing to the fact that there is a phenomenal amount of etheric force there, especially in the neighbourhood of California. I was shown a picture of the horoscope of this great country which was evidently not any of those hitherto published, and I gathered that the correct time of the nativity would never be known while there was any possibility of such knowledge being exploited for selfish ends.[1]

Amongst other interesting points it was apparent to me that a certain Saturnian aspect in the radical map had become temporarily strengthened through the progressed horoscope, causing

---

" Mr. George Plummer of New York has very kindly sent me a copy of his magazine, *Mercury*, in which appeared an article collecting various conflicting statements as to the date upon which the United States was born. Quite apart from any question as to the time of day, it would appear that there are excellent reasons for choosing either the 2nd, 4th, or 8th July, 1776 ; 2nd August, 1776 ; 15th November, 1777 ; or 21st June, 1788, as the correct birth-date. Therefore I can only warn readers not to accept any horoscope they see as indisputably that of the United States."—Vivian E. Robson, B.Sc., January, 1933, *The British Journal of Astrology*.

the more puritanical of the race to *enforce* prohibition. I saw that the Race Devas had hoped to make the country as a whole acquiescent to this innovation in order to raise the race to a higher subdivision of the physical ether. This new law was an expression of the powerful Saturnian element in the radical horoscope, whilst the failure and set-back materialised through a malefic aspect between certain planets in the elements air and water. The effort to enforce discipline from without, so typical of Saturnian psychology, proved abortive, and only became the instrument for the Dark Forces to throw the race back into even denser matter than before.

It was clear to me that the position of the planets gave the greatest possible activity in the water and air elements and their appropriate subdivisions of the ether. But whilst at the present time the majority of the race would appear to be almost over-stimulated by the vitality in the etheric element, I saw that this will no longer be the case when the higher types have acquired the new method of vitalisation and control of their etheric centres by means of those etheric forces associated with the planet Uranus, which rules the United States.

I was impressed to notice that this etheric

development of the future will entail a study of the ductless glands and their close relationship with the four subdivisions of the ether, for it will have become generally recognised that man's spiritual as well as his physical possibilities depend very largely upon the secretions of these organs. It was shown to me that those who had misused the sex-force in their immediate past lives were only capable of responding to the lowest sub-divisions of physical-etheric matter, and to that but inadequately. The idea of gland-grafting from animals will be looked upon with horror as it will be fully realised that the vital force lies in the ether interpenetrating the gland and *not* in the gland itself. Moreover, the mere fact of grafting or administering a gland from an animal only tends to cut off the higher self from the physical body, owing to the rate of vibration that separates the man from the beast.

I saw that the whole development of the future race will entail a complete co-ordination of the ductless glands ; but that *only* those who had acquired some measure of self-control through clean living in past lives would have the etheric body requisite for this achievement.

As Uranus for the majority will have greater affinity with the pineal gland than the Sun, the whole procedure of co-relating the ductless glands with the physical etheric body will start with the head, and descend into the subconscious by means of the fourth or Uranian subdivision of the ether.[1] When the subconscious mind has yielded up all its secrets and is *entirely* under the control of the will, the life-force will become quickened and ascend through the third or Jupiterian subdivision, and the future initiate will comprehend the mystery of the dual sign Gemini and acquire the power to control the cerebro-spinal system under the direction of his Master.[2] At a *much later date* the ductless glands associated with the sign Libra, which rules the back and is the key to the control of the sympathetic system, will become vitalised by the second or Neptunian subdivision of the ether and the Coming Race will then combine the masculine and feminine forces in one body. I further perceived that the first or Solar subdivision of the ether hitherto associated with the awakening of Kundalini had *no* part in this new development, and will still

[1] This method of development will become a part of the lesser mysteries on the inner planes during the Uranian decanate of the Aquarian Age.

[2] Those who have affinity with Gemini will attempt to master the mystery of this sign. Other types will co-relate the Jupiterian sub-division of the ether with the sign Sagittarius and become proficient mediums for the Masters along various lines of co-operative work.

F

remain a mystery involving the relationship between the Master and His advanced Chelas.

With the conquest of the airy subdivision of the ether, the transference of thought-vibrations will become as much a commonplace as is the transference of sound-vibrations at the present day. The influence of both Uranus and Neptune will be responsible for stimulating this new form of mental-etheric activity. By functioning positively and negatively in the airy subdivision of the ether, the Uranian type of man will become the perfect transmitter and the Neptunian the perfect sensitive receiving-station.

This power of thought-transference has always been practised by the Adepts as a means of communication with each other and Their pupils, and when brought to a state of perfection on the part of each individual, will imply the *equal* development of the Uranian power of transmission and the Neptunian. power of reception.[1]

At the present time my own Master is the

[1] " Among the advantages of Yoga is included the possibility of intercourse with the Teachers. In this regard one must distinguish two types of current. The isolated current and the *current of space*. The isolated current responds to the *one* chosen Teacher. The current of space permits one not only the contact with many Teachers but gives also the possibility of receiving cosmic knowledge. It is necessary to realise the difference in the expenditure of forces in both currents. As a lamp is affected by various currents, so the *centres* vibrate to the currents of space. Verily caution is needed to bring into daily life the combination of such varied energies."—*Agni Yoga.*

most brilliant exponent of this dual power, and
is known as the *Adept of the Ether* by His Peers,
Who look to Him to elucidate the most abstruse
problems in connection with the cosmic ether interpenetrating space far beyond our Solar System.

Ever since the Lunation of January, 1910,
when Uranus and Neptune were in opposition
to each other and also afflicting Mars, Saturn and
Jupiter, their enigmatical influence has constituted
an object of study and meditation for every
member of the Hierarchy. The vibrations of
Uranus and Neptune which in natures unevolved
and uncontrolled are liable to produce such dis-
cord and such chaos, are utilised by the Great
Ones, in Whom they become perfectly synthesised,
for purposes of transmutation, harmonisation and
reconstruction.[1]

Their intense concentration upon the solution
of common problems unites Them to each other
more closely than ever, and even tends to create a
certain facial resemblance between Them which
is especially apparent in the expression of the eyes.

Foremost among the many intricate types of
activity upon which Their attention is focussed,

[1] " The spheres of psychic energy penetrate all obstacles. All
physical and mechanical manifestations have no value, in com-
parison with the finest energy, and the whole future is founded
upon the highest energies, upon the return of coarse matter into
the domain of light."—*Agni Yoga*.

and which is possible alone through contacting the highest vibrations of Neptune, is that species of psychological identification previously alluded to in connection with Master Koot Hoomi. Not only He, but Others, are adopting this procedure which enables Them in a new and subtle manner to enter into the consciousness of Their pupils, and indeed of all who respond to these planetary influences.

Thus will the Great Ones in a sense walk the earth again, merged in the consciousness of Their pupils, sharing the difficulties and the problems of their daily life. And if it be objected that such a descent into the sordid and the trivial is derogatory to the status and dignity of such august Beings, it should be borne in mind that this power to descend into greater depths inevitably carries with it the power to rise to greater heights ; and that by this close and intimate identification the Adepts are not only better able to guide, to console and to inspire Their loved ones in the material worlds, but to identify Themselves with the consciousness of those wondrous Entities—Cosmic Devas, Rulers of far-off Systems—to union with Whom They in love, in reverence, in adoration, aspire even as we so aspire to union with our Masters.

APPENDIX

ANNIE BESANT'S PLANETS
IN RELATIONSHIP TO THE HOROSCOPE
OF THE SOCIETY

ASTROLOGICAL CHART

Name: Theosophical Society

Date: 17th November   **Time:** 8 p.m.

New York   1875

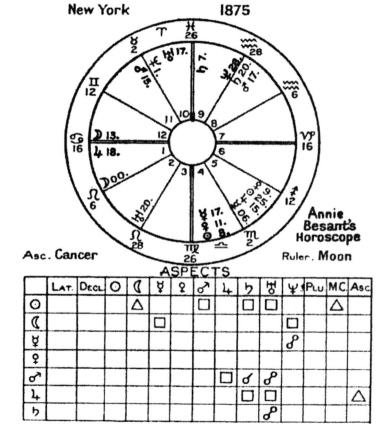

Annie Besant's Horoscope

Asc. Cancer

Ruler. Moon

ASPECTS

	Lat.	Decl.	☉	☽	☿	♀	♂	♃	♄	♅	♆	Plu	MC	Asc
☉				△			□		□	□				△
☽			□							□				
☿									☍					
♀														
♂							□	♂	☍					△
♃								□	□					△
♄									☍					

ANNIE BESANT'S PLANETS IN RELATION-
SHIP TO THE HOROSCOPE OF THE
SOCIETY

The reason why the Society increased in numbers and general recognition from the time that Dr. Annie Besant became president, is obvious from the fact that her planets formed benefic aspects to its radical horoscope, involving the first, fourth, ninth and tenth houses. These aspects produced good mundane conditions and inspired numerous activities for all concerned. Likewise her Mercury, forming a sextile to the radical Uranus, created a condition of trust in her integrity, so that money flowed into the Society, despite the bad financial aspects resulting from the afflicted Uranus in the second house of the radical figure.

It is not until we study the ninth house that we see the first sign of inner conflict and subtle difficulties, the grappling with which was *indefinitely postponed*. This situation arose because her Neptune was square the radical Sun in Scorpio, causing a persistent inability to co-relate past occult traditions with the psychological development of the day, a problem which must presumably remain to be worked out in some other life, since it involves the *ninth house*, the house of the future. As her Saturn was in benefic aspect to the radical Mercury and Jupiter, Annie Besant was always happiest and most successful in expounding truth by means of broad generalisations. Her Uranus forming strong aspects from the tenth house of the Society, galvanised it into fiery enthusiasm, always associated with the sign Aries. Obviously devoid of all baser personal desires, she was able to inspire both spiritual and mundane activities. Her inability to train her followers to take over the work she had begun, is shown through her Mars in Taurus forming malefic aspects from the eleventh house to the radical Uranus, Saturn, Mars and Jupiter. These afflictions resulted in financial waste and incapacity to fulfil occult discipline, as well as in creating sex difficulties among her co-workers and subordinates.

Her ideals, traditions and capacity for gruelling work were the best attributes of a past generation, but the younger members of the Society, disillusioned by the war and its aftermath, were out of sympathy with her point of view, and became chiefly concerned with the discovery of the subconscious mind, which Annie Besant, however, as president of the Society, refused to consider in relationship to that organisation.

Dimly realising that the elements fire, air and water in cardinal signs were all afflicting each other in her own horoscope, she sought escape in extraversion, through her ruler Mars in the *first* house, her only planet free from affliction. Her third and ninth houses being without strong planetary influences, she was not equipped for new lines of psychological thought, and equally unable to intuit the emotional difficulties of another generation.

C. W. LEADBEATER'S PLANETS
IN RELATIONSHIP TO THE HOROSCOPE
OF THE SOCIETY

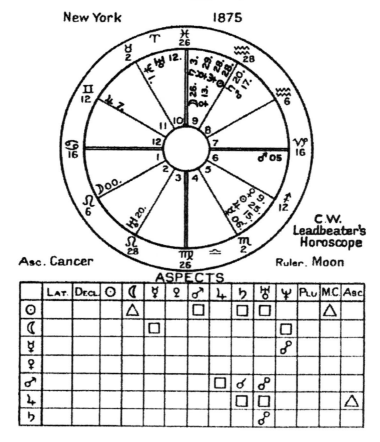

ASTROLOGICAL CHART

NAME: Theosophical Society

DATE: 17th November   TIME: 8 p.m.

New York   1875

Asc. Cancer

C.W.
Leadbeater's
Horoscope

Ruler. Moon

ASPECTS

	LAT.	DECL.	☉	☽	☿	♀	♂	♃	♄	♅	♆	PLU.	M.C.	Asc
☉				△			□		□	□			△	
☽			□								□			
☿											☍			
♀														
♂							□	☌	☍					
♃									□	□				△
♄										☍				

C. W. LEADBEATER'S PLANETS IN RELATIONSHIP TO THE HOROSCOPE OF THE SOCIETY

No less than six of C. W. Leadbeater's planets influence the ninth house of the Theosophical nativity, thereby indicating the strong higher mental influence he has had over that organisation. His Neptune, Mercury and Sun, in exact conjunction with Annie Besant's Neptune, and forming the same square to the radical Sun, were the cause of most of her difficulties within the Society. These difficulties were accentuated through his Sun and Neptune being in opposition to the radical Uranus, and his Jupiter afflicting the radical Venus, aspects which created conditions strong enough to arouse considerable criticism on the part of the outside world as well as on that of the Society itself.

His Moon on the cusp of the radical *midheaven*, in trine to the radical Sun, enabled him not only to remain in the Society, but to dominate

its activities for many years, whilst the favourable
progressed Jupiter also in trine to his radical
Moon, allowed his personality to benefit from as
well as chiefly *direct* the Society along ceremonial
lines.　Having so many planets in Pisces, and
even Saturn, the depositor of the three influences
in Aquarius, being also in that sign, he inevitably
visualised the future activities of the Seventh Ray
in terms of Christianity and Masonry, although
these activities were essentially those of the
passing Age.　This tendency on his part became
more and more marked in later years as his personality responded increasingly to the progressed
Jupiter aspect of the Society, forming from the
fifth house, the house of the past.

His next life should come under the influence of
Saturn, which, being in the sign Pisces, suggests
further karma to be worked out in connection
with the thought-currents he created for so many
by his powerful personality, so largely coloured
by the influence of the passing Age.

KRISHNAMURTI'S HOROSCOPE
IN RELATIONSHIP TO THE SOCIETY

ASTROLOGICAL CHART

Name: Theosophical Society

Date: 17th November   **Time:** 8 p.m.

New York   1875

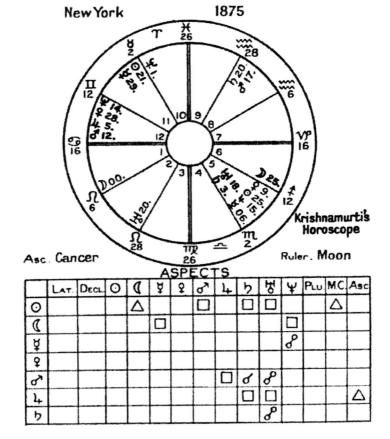

Krishnamurti's Horoscope

Asc. Cancer   Ruler. Moon

ASPECTS

	Lat.	Decl.	☉	☽	☿	♀	♂	♃	♄	♅	♆	Plu.	M.C.	Asc
☉				△			□		□	□			△	
☽					□						□			
☿										☍				
♀														
♂							□	☌	☍					△
♃								□	□					
♄									☍					

KRISHNAMURTI'S HOROSCOPE IN RELA-
TION TO THE SOCIETY

It will immediately be seen that the majority
of Krishnamurti's planets fall in the twelfth
house of the Theosophical nativity, the house of
introspection and self-undoing. His Jupiter and
Mars are in benefic aspect to the radical Mercury
and Jupiter respectively. Through these planetary forces he was able to influence certain members
of the Society who were sufficiently self-conscious
to intuit the particular form of introversion his
message demanded. For the rest, the numerous
oppositions and squares formed between the two
horoscopes created temporary havoc, involving
past occult traditions, prevailing activities and
even financial difficulties. His Moon, separating
from the trine of Uranus in the radical house of
finance, shows the pecuniary aid which he
received through the Society during his youth and
early manhood ; but the fact that the radical
Saturn and Uranus afflicted his ascendant, was
responsible for his subsequent phase of refusing

to benefit through the Society either in a spiritual or a mundane sense.

Yet in spite of all the conflict involved, his remarkable personality created a new self-conscious current of thought within the Society, through the sextile which his Moon, in the intuitive sign Sagittarius, forms to the cusp of the radical ninth house ruled by Aquarius, the sign of the New Age. Through this aspect he *escaped* out of immediate difficulties into a state of consciousness wholly impersonal, from which problems, both psychological and material, pressing enough for the majority, appear as mere fantasies. Nevertheless, the fact that the sign Scorpio rules the house of the future in Krishnamurti's own map and contains Saturn and Uranus, the latter afflicted, is an indication that in his next life he may become involved in those very psychological problems which he has either evaded or ignored in this incarnation. For those who have Saturn in the ninth house usually in the present life generate fresh karma which must perforce be worked out in another incarnation under the limitations of this particular planet.

H. P. BLAVATSKY'S HOROSCOPE
IN RELATIONSHIP TO THE THEOSOPHICAL
SOCIETY

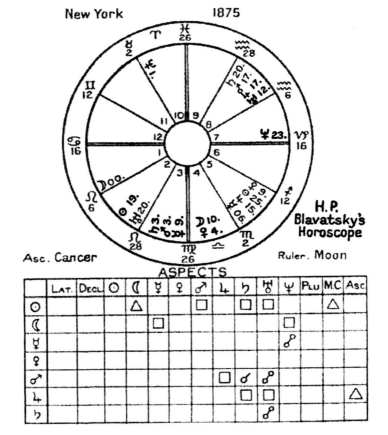

ASTROLOGICAL CHART

NAME: Theosophical Society

DATE: 17th November   **TIME:** 8 p.m.

New York   1875

H. P. Blavatsky's Horoscope

Asc. Cancer   Ruler. Moon

ASPECTS

	Lat.	Decl.	☉	☽	☿	♀	♂	♃	♄	♅	♆	Plu	MC	Asc
☉				△			□		□	□			△	
☽					□					□				
☿										☍				
♀														
♂							□	☌	☍					△
♃									□	□				△
♄										☍				

H. P. BLAVATSKY'S HOROSCOPE IN RELATIONSHIP TO THE THEOSOPHICAL SOCIETY

The planet Uranus was in its own sign Aquarius and in the eighth house in the horoscope of H. P. Blavatsky. This position conveys that she was expressed through this planet chiefly along occult lines and that she is likely to be even more under its influence in her next life, since the sign Aquarius rules the cusp of her ninth house according to one nativity.* This position of Uranus in Aquarius is an indication that the Master Koot Hoomi, with whom she had such a close rapport, may again use her as His medium through their mutual close association with this sign. H. P. Blavatsky's Sun being in the fiery sign Leo, and therefore vitalising the planets in Aquarius and Scorpio of the Theosophical nativity, would seem to denote that she will return to the world during the thirty-year Aquarian cycle of that organisation. Her ruler, the Moon, in conjunction with Venus in the fourth house,

* The exact time of H. P. Blavatsky's birth is not known.

indicates the same maternal protective feeling for the Society as possessed by Annie Besant, whose Venus is in a similar position.

The position of Neptune in H. P. Blavatsky's sixth house was responsible both for her phenomena and for the illnesses which frequently arose through so much exhaustion of etheric force. Having a later degree of Cancer rising at birth than that of the Society, her Neptune fell in its seventh house, forming benefic aspects to the radical Sun, to the cusp of the mid-heaven and to the cusp of the fourth house ; all these aspects clearly show her inspiring and preserving influence over the movement whilst she was in incarnation, and the strong probability of her continuing the same work under a powerful Neptune influence, which will again cause her to be in advance of her time. Her basic ideas of occultism having become more or less accepted, it will remain for her to apply the ancient science to modern problems during the minor Aquarian Cycle.

CPSIA information can be obtained at www.ICGtesting.com
Printed in the USA
LVOW052028020613

336549LV00001B/204/P

9 781578 632046